Animals in Danger

in Europe

Louise and Richard Spilsbury

Heinemann
LIBRARY
Chicago, Illinois

Edited by Rebecca Rissman, Dan Nunn, and Adrian Vigliano
Designed by Philippa Jenkins
Picture research by Tracy Cummins
Originated by Capstone Global Library Ltd.
Printed in China by South China Printing Company, Ltd.

17 16 15 14 13
10 9 8 7 6 5 4 3 2 1

Library of Congress Cataloging-in-Publication Data
Cataloging-in-Publication data is on file at the Library of Congress.
ISBN: 978-1-4329-7675-0 (HC) 978-1-4329-7682-8 (PB)

Acknowledgments
The author and publisher are grateful to the following for permission to reproduce copyright material: Alamy pp. 17, 19 (© blickwinkel), 21 (© Chris Gomersall); Filipe Lopes p. 13 (© Filipe Lopes); Getty Images p. 29 (Catherine Ledner); istockphoto p. 11 (© Merlin Farwell); National Geographic Stock p. 26 (JOEL SARTORE); Nature Picture Library p. 27 (© Igor Shpilenok); NHPA pp. 22 (Hellio & Van Ingen), 25 (Dhritiman Mukherjee); Shutterstock pp. 4 (© Chris P.), 5 bottom (© Aleksander Bolbot), 5 top (© dimitris_k), 6 (© Christian Musat), 15 (© Rafa Irusta), 23 (©Peter Leahy), 28 (© Roca), icons (© Florian Augustin), (© tristan tan), maps (© AridOcean); Superstock pp. 9, 10, 14 (© NHPA), 18 (© Minden Pictures).

Cover photograph alpine ibex produced with permission of Shutterstock (© Peter Wey).
Cover photograph of a European bison reproduced with permission of Shutterstock (© MilousSK).
Cover photograph of a bluefin tuna reproduced with permission of Shutterstock (© holbox).
Cover photograph of a bluefin tuna in net reproduced with permission of istockphoto (© Gary Stokes).
Cover photograph of a Spanish lynx reproduced with permission of Superstock (© Minden Pictures).
Cover photograph of a herd of European bison reproduced with permission of istockphoto (© Linda More).

We would like to thank Michael Bright for his invaluable help in the preparation of this book.

Every effort has been made to contact copyright holders of any material reproduced in this book. Any omissions will be rectified in subsequent printings if notice is given to the publisher.

All the Internet addresses (URLs) given in this book were valid at the time of going to press. However, due to the dynamic nature of the Internet, some addresses may have changed, or sites may have changed or ceased to exist since publication. While the author and publisher regret any inconvenience this may cause readers, no responsibility for any such changes can be accepted by either the author or the publisher.

Contents

Some words are shown in bold, **like this.** You can find out what they mean by looking in the glossary.

Where Is Europe?

We divide the world into seven large areas of land called **continents**. Europe is the second-smallest continent. Europe has a large area of mainland and many islands, such as the United Kingdom.

NORTH AMERICA

EUROPE

ASIA

ATLANTIC OCEAN

AFRICA

PACIFIC OCEAN

PACIFIC OCEAN

SOUTH AMERICA

INDIAN OCEAN

AUSTRALIA

N

W   E

S

ANTARCTICA

Can you see the continent of Europe?

There are many types of **habitat** in Europe. There are long rivers, high mountains, rolling hills, leafy woodlands, and areas of open **plains**. There is also a large area of coastline.

Many animals live in Europe's different habitats.

Animals of Europe

Some animals in Europe are **endangered**. This means there are very few of that type of animal left. If they all die, that type of animal will be **extinct**. An animal that is extinct is gone from the planet forever!

The red squirrel is endangered in the United Kingdom and could be extinct in less than 10 years.

Different types of animals look and behave differently from each other. We sort them into groups to help tell them apart.

Animal Classification Chart

Amphibian	• lives on land and in water • has damp, smooth skin • has **webbed** feet • lays many eggs
Bird	• has feathers and wings • hatches out of hard-shelled eggs
Fish	• lives in water • has **fins** and most have **scales** • young hatch from soft eggs
Mammal	• drinks milk when a baby • has hair on its body
Reptile	• has scales on its body • lives on land • young hatch from soft-shelled eggs

Look out for pictures like these next to each photo. They will tell you what type of animal each photo shows.

The United Kingdom

Some of the United Kingdom's **endangered** animals live in woodlands and **wetlands**. Wetlands are areas of shallow water by trees. People destroy these **habitats** for wood, for farmland, and to build on.

This map shows some of the United Kingdom's wild places.

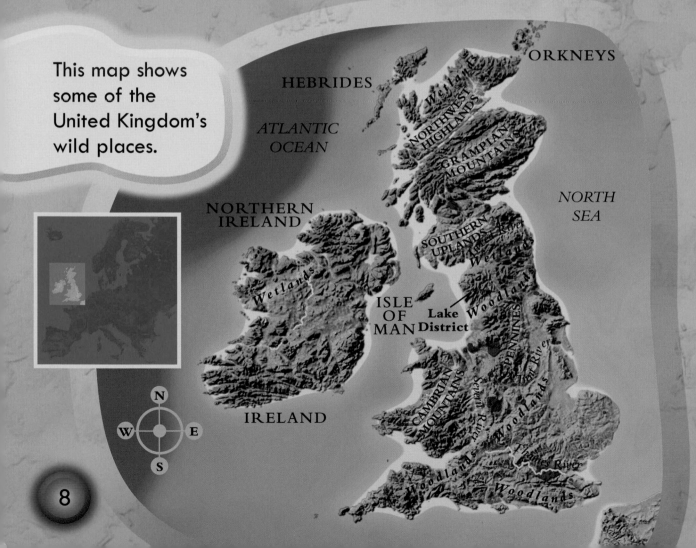

ORKNEYS

HEBRIDES

ATLANTIC OCEAN

Wetlands

NORTHWEST HIGHLANDS

GRAMPIAN MOUNTAINS

NORTH SEA

NORTHERN IRELAND

SOUTHERN UPLANDS

Tweed River

Wetlands

Wetlands

ISLE OF MAN

Lake District

Woodlands

PENNINES

Tees River

CAMBRIAN MOUNTAINS

Severn River

Woodlands

IRELAND

N W E S

Thames River

Woodlands

Woodlands

Dormice need trees to survive. They sleep in trees during the day and feed in trees at night. In autumn, they fill up on fruit, nuts, and **insects** and sleep all winter in nests made of **bark** and grass!

Dormice spend up to three-quarters of their life asleep!

Scottish wild cats live in woodlands. During the day, they rest in trees, old fox dens, and on rocks. They hunt for rabbits or young deer at dawn and dusk. Females have up to eight kittens every year!

Wild cat kittens can hiss and spit at things that upset them after they are a week old!

A bitterns' brown feathers help it to hide from **predators** in muddy wetlands.

Bitterns need wetlands to survive. They hunt for fish in the shallow water. Males make loud booming noises to attract females to lay eggs here, too. They can be heard from several miles away!

Western Europe

Some **endangered** animals in western Europe live on islands around the long coastline, in mountains, or in woodlands.

Part of Western Europe is a peninsula, which is a long area of land surrounded by water.

ATLANTIC OCEAN

Loire River

AZORES

MADEIRA

CANARY ISLANDS

CANTABRIAN MOUNTAINS

Woodlands

Woodlands

Douro River

Tagus River

Woodlands

PYRENEES MOUNTAINS

N
W   E
S

The Azorean bat rests in trees, buildings, and caves on the Azores islands at night. It is one of the only bats that hunt for **insects** during the day. **Predators** do not try to catch it during the day!

The Azorean bat is endangered because people disturb its **roosts** and cut down trees.

The Montseny brook newt lives in cold, fast-flowing mountain streams. Its skin has poisons that stop predators from eating it. Its **habitats** are drying up because people take the water to sell in bottles.

This newt's bright colors warn predators that it has poisonous skin!

This lynx climbs and swims well and travels far each day in search of food.

The Iberian lynx uses its sharp eyesight and huge, tufted ears to locate **prey**. It mainly eats rabbits, usually one a day! When people clear its forest habitat for farmland, it has fewer rabbits to eat.

Central and Northern Europe

Some **endangered** animals in central and northern Europe live in woodlands and rivers. People destroy animal homes when they cut down trees, and they disturb animals by building **dams** on rivers.

This map shows central and northern Europe.

N
W E
S

NORWEGIAN SEA

KJØLEN MOUNTAINS

Woodlands

Woodlands

Woodlands

Elbe River

Rhine River

Dnieper River

CARPATHIAN MOUNTAINS

Woodlands

ALPS

Danube River

BLACK SEA

The European bison is the biggest, heaviest mammal in Europe, but it can still jump over streams and run fast! It needs woodlands to survive because it eats leaves, trees, **bark**, and berries from trees.

Bison are as tall as a man and live in groups called **herds**.

In rivers, young eels feed on small animals at night and rest in mud during the day.

Young European eels hatch from eggs in the ocean and drift into rivers, where they feed and grow. Later, adults swim to the ocean, have young, and die. Some get trapped in dams on their journey.

The Danube salmon is a fierce fish! It catches all kinds of river animals in its mouth full of sharp, cone-shaped teeth. Dams stop it from swimming to areas in which it usually lays eggs.

This huge salmon can grow to 6 feet (1.8 meters) in length—as long as a man!

Southern Europe

Southern Europe is a warm, sunny area. People disturb some animals here by visiting or building on the coast or on the inland **wetlands**. People also harm animals by dropping trash in the sea.

Woodlands
Woodlands
Woodlands
Woodlands
Po River
Danube River
BLACK SEA
Wetlands
APENNINES
CORSICA
BALEARIC ISLANDS
SARDINIA
SICILY
MEDITERRANEAN SEA
CRETE
CYPRUS
N
W
E
S

This map shows southern Europe.

The slender-billed curlew pulls **prey** from the mud with its long, curved beak!

The slender-billed curlew wades slowly through wetlands. It pecks at the mud to find worms, **insects**, and shellfish to eat. People hunted it for food and are now taking over its wetland **habitats**, too!

The Mediterranean monk seal feeds on fish and octopus. Then it comes onto beaches to rest. People take over the beaches, so it has nowhere to rest. Fishermen also kill the seal to stop it from eating fish.

These seals are some of the most **endangered** mammals in the world.

Some sea turtles get hit by boats when they swim to the surface to breathe.

The loggerhead turtle's strong **jaws** crush shellfish, crabs, and jellyfish. Sadly, some turtles die when they mistake floating plastic bags for jellyfish. Some drown when they get tangled in fishing nets.

23

Eastern Europe

In eastern Europe, there are mountains, rivers, and open **plains** with areas of **wetlands**. People take over plains and **drain** wetlands for farming. They catch animals for food and **pollute** rivers, too.

There are many mountains in eastern Europe.

Grasslands

Grasslands

Danube River

Grasslands

CARPATHIAN MOUNTAINS

Wetlands

SEA OF AZOV

CAUCASUS

TRANSYLVANIAN ALPS

BLACK SEA

BALKAN MOUNTAINS

N
W E
S

MEDITERRANEAN SEA

The sociable lapwing feeds and nests on open land. It walks along, picking up **insects** to eat. It lays eggs in dips in the soil. People take the land the sociable lapwing lives on for farming, and farm animals trample lapwing nests.

At 16 feet (5 meters) long, the beluga sturgeon is the biggest fish in Europe's rivers! It swims into rivers to lay its eggs on rocks. People take these eggs to sell as an expensive food called caviar.

The barbels in front of the sturgeon's mouth feel for fish and other **prey** on the riverbed.

The desman uses its **webbed** feet to paddle along and its long nose as a snorkel!

The Russian desman eats fish, insects, and other prey, but it is at risk from habitat loss. It is also eaten by animals such as mink, which people put in rivers to catch for their fur.

27

H lp in -uro ' Animal

Some countries in Europe protect animals in **reserves**. These are places where animals can live safely. Hunting nearly made the Alpine ibex **extinct,** but now it lives safely in the Alps.

The alpine ibex is a wild goat that lives in the mountains of the Alps.

You can help **endangered** animals, too! Try not to disturb animals when you are walking in nature, and don't drop litter. Animals can get trapped in it or harmed when they swallow it.

Why not help animals by helping at a local litter clean-up?

Glossary

bark outer covering of a tree

continent one of seven large areas that make up the world's land

dam barrier that holds back water on a river

drain to cause water to leave something, like a pond

endangered when a type of animal is in danger of dying out

extinct no longer alive; not seen in the wild for 50 years

fin flat body part that sticks out of a fish's body and helps it steer and move

habitat place where plants and animals live

herd group of animals

insect small animal with six legs, such as an ant or fly

jaws part of an animal's body that contains its mouth and teeth

plain large area of flat land with few trees

pollute to poison or damage air, water, or land

predator animal that catches and eats other animals for food

prey animal that gets caught and eaten by other animals

reserve large area of land where plants and animals are protected

roost place where bats and birds sleep or rest

scale small, overlapping pieces that cover an animal's body

webbed when feet have skin between the toes

wetland land covered in shallow water

Find Out More

Books

Allgor, Marie. *Endangered Animals of Europe*. New York: PowerKids Press, 2011.

Kalman, Bobbie. *Why Do Animals Become Extinct?* New York: Crabtree Publishing Co., 2012.

Internet sites

Facthound offers a safe, fun way to find web sites related to this book. All the sites on Facthound have been researched by our staff.

Here's all you do:
Visit www.facthound.com
Type in this code: 9781432976750

Index